101 Quick & Easy

Pasta Recipes

Victoria Steele

Cooking 101 - Quick & Easy

COOKBOOK series

ISBN: 9781092644501

CONTENTS

Pasta with Sauce _____ 9

Bow Ties with Artichoke Sauce _____ 9

Simple Garlic Parmesan Fettuccine _____ 10

Spaghetti with Herbs, Tomatoes and Cheese _____ 11

Egg Noodles _____ 12

Italian Turkey Meatballs with Mostaccioli _____ 13

Greek Pasta _____ 14

Fettuccine Florentine _____ 15

Orlando Mostaccioli and Meatballs _____ 16

Pasta Palermo _____ 18

Rigatoni with Sausage Sauce _____ 19

Fettuccine A La Crème _____ 20

Spaghetti Al Pomodoro _____ 21

Simple Classic Alfredo _____ 22

Fettuccine with Wilted Escarole and Mushrooms ___ 23

Pistachio Pasta _____ 24

Fettuccine with Gorgonzola _____ 25

Linguine and Mushrooms _____ 26

Steak Italiano _____ 27

Black Pepper Fettuccine with Veal, Peas and Cream __ 28

Macaroni and Garbanzos _____ 29

Quick & Easy Hamburger Casserole _____ 30

Baked Pasta _____ 31

Vermicelli Casserole _____ 31

Baked Mostaccioli _____ 32

Macaroni Au Gratin _____ 33

Ziti with Three Cheeses _____ 34

Lasagna Rolls _____ 35

Macaroni and Cheese _____ 36

Italian Hot Dish _____ 37

Spicy Ziti _____ 38

Baked Penne and Smoked Sausage _____ 39

Macaroni Bake _____ 40

Pepperoni Casserole _____ 41

Spicy Rigatoni Bake _____ 42

Italian Casserole _____ 43

Crockpot Macaroni and Cheese _____ 44

Grandma's Scalloped Corn _____ 45

Macaroni Hamburger Casserole _____ 46

Lazy Lasagna _____ 47

Lasagna Cordon Blue _____ 48

Mushroom Lasagna _____ 49

Lasagna Florentine _____ 50

Baked Spaghetti with Mushroom Soup _____ 52

Pirogies _____ 53

Macaroni Loaf _____ 54

Easy Spaghetti Pie _____ 55

Macaroni Pizza _____ 56

Crunchy Ham Casserole _____ 57

Stuffed Pasta _____ 58

Ham-Stuffed Manicotti with Cheese Sauce _____ 58

Tortellini and Spinach Pasta _____ 59

Ravioli _____ 60

Cannelloni _____ 62

Tortellini Bake _____ 64

Manicotti with Cheese Filling _____ 65

Stuffed Jumbo Shells _____ 66

Pasta with Poultry _____ 67

Chicken with Sun Dried Tomatoes _____ 67

Angel Hair Pasta Chicken Lo Mein _____ 68

Chicken Marinara _____ 69

Turkey Tetrazzini _____ 70

Chicken Casserole Supreme _____ 71

Rotel Chicken _____ 72

Chicken-Spaghetti Casserole _____ 73

20-Minute Stovetop Chicken Parmesan _____ 74

Easy Chicken Casserole _____ 75

Fish and Seafood with Pasta _____ 76

Buttery Pasta with Shrimp _____ 76

Broccoli-Shrimp Sauce for Pasta _____ 77

Cold Fettuccine with Shrimp _____ 78

Imitation Crab and Artichoke Casserole _____ 79

Pasta Soups _____ 80

Chicken Soup with Vermicelli _____ 80

Vegetable Soup _____ 81

Slow Cooker Pasta Vegetable Soup _____ 82

Minestrone Soup _____ 83

Hearty Minestrone Soup _____84

Tortellini Soup _____85

Italian Sausage Soup _____86

Pasta and Bean Soup _____87

Pepperoni Bow Tie Soup _____88

Chunky Pork Soup _____89

*Pasta Salads and Side Dishes*_____**90**

Vermicelli Salad with Crabmeat _____90

Light and Easy Pasta Salad_____91

Pizza Salad _____92

Fire and Ice Pasta Salad _____93

Best Pasta Salad_____94

Greek Rotini Salad _____95

Penne Pasta Salad _____96

Piquant Vermicelli _____97

Rigatoni Salad _____98

Cashew Tortellini Chicken Salad _____99

Shrimp Salad _____100

Green Tomato Pasta _____101

Ham, Peas and Cheese Salad_____102

Shrimp Salad _____103

Armenian Pilaf _____104

Ham and Macaroni Salad _____105

Acini De Pepe Pasta Fruit Salad_____106

Macaroni Fruit Salad _____107

Italian Pasta Salad _____108

Macaroni and Chicken Salad _____109

Hearty Macaroni Salad _____110

Spring Salad with Shell Pasta _____111

Smoked Turkey and Pepper Pasta Salad _____112

Tomato Spaghetti Salad _____113

Guidance for Dry Pasta vs. Cooked Pasta

Type of Pasta	Uncooked Amount	Cooked Amount
Angel Hair	8 ounces	4 cups
Bow Tie Pasta	8 ounces	4 cups
Egg Noodle	8 ounces	4 cups
Elbow Macaroni	8 ounces	4 cups
Fettuccine	8 ounces	3-1/4 cups
Linguine	8 ounces	4 cups
Rigatoni	8 ounces	4 cups
Rotini	8 ounces	4-1/2 cups
Spaghetti	8 ounces	5 cups
Vermicelli	8 ounces	4-1/2 cups
Ziti	8 ounces	4-1/2 cups

Victoria Steele

Pasta with Sauce

Bow Ties with Artichoke Sauce

12 oz. bowtie pasta
2 tablespoons butter
1 tablespoon flour
1 1/2 cups half and half
1/2 cup fresh Parmesan cheese
1/8 teaspoon nutmeg
1/8 teaspoon black pepper
1 tablespoon chopped fresh rosemary or 1 teaspoon dried rosemary
1 (14 oz.) can artichoke hearts, drained and cut
1 cup seeded and chopped tomato

Cook pasta according to package directions; drain.

In a medium saucepan, make a roux with butter and flour. Stirring constantly, add half and half; cook until thickened. Add cheese, nutmeg, pepper, rosemary, artichokes and tomatoes. Stirring occasionally, simmer until heated. Mix with hot pasta.

Yield: 6 servings

Simple Garlic Parmesan Fettuccine

12 oz. fettuccine
2 cloves garlic, minced
3 tablespoons butter
1/4 cup low fat sour cream
1/4 cup whipping cream
1/4 teaspoon salt
1/8 teaspoon black pepper
1/2 cup low-sodium chicken broth
1 cup shredded Parmesan cheese

Cook fettuccine according to directions on package; drain.

In small saucepan, sauté garlic in butter for 1 minute. In a small bowl, combine sour cream, whipping cream, salt and pepper. Add cream mixture and chicken broth to butter. Heat until hot but do not boil. Add fettuccine to cream sauce and stir in Parmesan cheese.

Yield: 6 servings

Spaghetti with Herbs, Tomatoes and Cheese

8 oz. spaghetti
2 tablespoons olive oil
1 small clove garlic, minced
3 medium tomatoes, diced
2 teaspoons basil
1/2 teaspoon salt
1 (4 oz.) pkg. reduced fat shredded mozzarella cheese
1/4 cup grated Parmesan cheese

Cook spaghetti according to package directions; drain.

Heat oil and sauté garlic. Stir in tomatoes, basil, salt and heat through. Add drained spaghetti; toss and add cheese.

Yield: 3 to 4 servings

Egg Noodles

These noodles can be served with spaghetti, Alfredo or butter sauce.

1 1/4 cups flour
1/2 teaspoon salt
1 egg yolk
1 egg
1/4 cup water
Extra flour, for dusting

In a large bowl, combine flour and salt. In a small bowl, mix egg yolk, egg and water. Make a well in the flour and add egg mixture; mix thoroughly until a stiff dough forms. Place dough on a floured surface and knead 10 minutes.

Bring a large stock pot of water to a boil. On a floured surface, roll out dough very thin; cut into strips. Place all noodles into boiling water and cook 10 to 15 minutes. Drain in colander and serve with desired sauce.

Yield: 4 to 6 servings

Italian Turkey Meatballs with Mostaccioli

1 (16 oz.) pkg. mostaccioli

Meatballs:

1 (9 oz.) pkg. frozen spinach, thawed
2 lb. ground turkey
6 slices cooked turkey bacon, crumbled
2 garlic cloves, minced
1 oz. (1/4 cup) fresh Parmesan cheese
3/4 cup Italian-style bread crumbs
2 eggs, beaten

Drain water from thawed spinach. Squeeze to remove as much liquid as possible. Mix ground turkey, bacon crumbles, garlic, cheese, bread crumbs and eggs with spinach. Form 1-1/2 inch balls; place in a single layer on a 10x15-inch ungreased baking sheet. Bake for 20 minutes at 350 degrees F. or until cooked through.

Cook pasta according to package directions; drain

Sauce:

1 (28 oz.) jar spaghetti sauce
1 (14.5 oz.) can Italian-style diced tomatoes, undrained
1 teaspoon granulated sugar
Fresh Parmesan cheese, shredded

Mix spaghetti sauce, tomatoes with liquid, sugar and; simmer until pasta and meatballs are ready to serve. Spoon over pasta and meatballs; garnish with shredded Parmesan cheese. Yield: 8 servings

Greek Pasta

1 lb. fettuccine
1 red bell pepper, julienned
1 yellow bell pepper, julienned
1 sweet onion, julienned
1 teaspoon olive oil
1/2 cup white wine
1 (14.5 oz.) can reduced-sodium chicken broth
1 teaspoon Greek seasoning
1/2 (6 oz.) container feta cheese
1/2 cup Parmesan cheese

Cook noodles according to package directions; drain.

Sauté red and yellow peppers and onion in olive oil until translucent. Add wine, chicken broth and Greek seasoning; heat to boiling. Reduce heat to low and add half of feta cheese. Remove from stove and add Parmesan cheese. Toss with pasta until coated.

Yield: 4 to 6 servings

Fettuccine Florentine

1 lb. fettuccine
1/2 cup butter
1 (10 oz.) package chopped spinach, thawed and drained, or fresh spinach, chopped
1 lb. bacon, crisply cooked and crumbled
1 1/2 cups heavy cream
1 egg, lightly beaten
2 cups (8 oz.) grated Parmesan cheese
Salt and pepper to taste

Cook fettuccine according to package directions; drain.

Melt butter in a large saucepan. Add spinach and bacon; sauté until spinach is wilted and hot. Add fettuccine and toss.

Combine cream and egg in a small bowl; pour over pasta. Add cheese and toss. Season with salt and pepper. Heat as needed, but do not cook.

Yield: 8 servings

Orlando Mostaccioli and Meatballs

Sauce:

1 to 2 pounds mild sausage (may substitute 1/2 hot and 1/2 sweet sausage)
1 tablespoon parsley
2 teaspoons oregano
1/8 teaspoon basil
6 (large) cloves garlic, minced
1 teaspoon salt
3 (29 oz. each) cans tomato puree
3 (6 oz.) cans tomato paste
1 onion, whole (outer skin removed)

Meatballs:

2 1/2 to 3 lb. ground beef
1 (1.5 oz.) package meat loaf seasoning mix
2 cloves garlic, finely chopped
1 tablespoon parsley
Salt and pepper, to taste
3 eggs, beaten
4 slices bread
1/2 cup milk
3/4 cup bread crumbs
6 oz. Parmesan cheese, grated

Pasta:

1 to 2 lb. mostaccioli (may substitute spaghetti)

To Make Sauce:

Brown sausage in large pot. Simmer, covered, about 30 minutes. Remove sausage, leaving fat for flavor. Stir in parsley, oregano, basil, garlic and salt. Add tomato puree and paste; mix well. Fill both puree and paste cans with water and add to sauce; mix well. Add whole onion (which will be removed just before serving). Simmer at least 2 hours.

To Make Meatballs:

In a large bowl, mix together ground beef, seasoning mix, garlic, parsley, salt, pepper and eggs.

In a small bowl, soak each slice of bread in the milk. Squeeze out excess milk and break bread apart into small pieces.

In a medium bowl, combine bread, bread crumbs and Parmesan cheese. Add to ground beef and mix thoroughly. Shape into small balls and cook in a skillet or bake at 350 degrees for 40 minutes. Add to sauce to serve.

To Make Pasta:

Prepare pasta according to package directions; drain and rinse in hot water. When serving, top with sauce.

Yield: 8 to 12 servings

Pasta Palermo

1 (16 oz.) pkg. spaghetti
1/2 cup olive oil
3 garlic cloves, crushed
1 cup sliced mushrooms
10 green olives, sliced
10 black olives, sliced
1 roasted red pepper, julienned
1/2 cup prosciutto, julienned
1/2 cup genoa or hard salami, julienned
1/3 cup grated Parmesan or Romano cheese

Cook spaghetti according to package directions; drain.

In a large skillet, heat olive oil and sauté garlic until it is golden. Remove garlic from the oil and discard. Add mushrooms, olives and roasted pepper. Sauté until mushrooms are cooked.

Add prosciutto and Genoa salami; heat through. Pour over spaghetti and toss in cheese. If needed, add more olive oil to the hot mixture.

Yield: 4 to 6 servings

Rigatoni with Sausage Sauce

1 (16 oz.) pkg. rigatoni
Romano cheese, grated

Sausage Sauce:

1 lb. bulk Italian sausage
1 onion, chopped
2 cloves garlic, minced
1 (14.5 oz.) can Italian tomatoes
1 (6 oz.) can tomato paste
1 (6 oz.) can of water
1/8 teaspoon oregano
2 fresh basil leaves or 1 teaspoon dry basil
2 (4 oz. each) cans mushrooms
1/8 teaspoon salt
1/4 teaspoon pepper

Cook rigatoni according to package directions; drain.

In a skillet, cook sausage, drain and reserve grease. Sauté onion and garlic in sausage grease until lightly browned.

In a large pot, combine sausage, onion, garlic, tomatoes and tomato paste, water, oregano, basil, mushrooms, salt and pepper. Simmer uncovered for 2 hours. Serve sauce over rigatoni noodles. Top with Romano cheese.

Yield: 4 servings

Fettuccine A La Crème

1 lb. fettuccine
1/2 cup butter
1 clove garlic
1/4 cup dry white wine or dry sherry
Salt and pepper to taste
2 tablespoons fresh parsley, chopped
1/2 teaspoon dried or 1 teaspoon fresh basil, chopped
1 cup heavy cream
1/2 cup grated Parmesan cheese
1 tablespoon chopped chives

Cook fettuccine according to package directions; drain.

Melt butter in a large skillet and sauté garlic for 3 to 4 minutes over low heat. Remove and discard garlic. Add wine, salt, pepper, parsley and basil to skillet; simmer 5 minutes. Add cream and heat just until hot (don't boil). Pour cream sauce and Parmesan cheese over noodles and mix. Garnish with chives.

Yield: 8 servings.

Spaghetti Al Pomodoro

1 (16 oz.) package angel hair pasta
4 tablespoons butter
1/4 cup onion, finely chopped
1/4 cup carrots, finely diced
1/4 cup celery, finely diced
2 cups (canned) whole peeled tomatoes, with juice, coarsely chopped
Salt to taste

Cook pasta according to package directions; drain.

Sauté onion, carrots and celery in butter until softened. Add tomatoes and salt; simmer 20 to 30 minutes. Serve over pasta.

Yield: 5 servings

Simple Classic Alfredo

1/2 (6 oz.) pkg. fettuccine
1/4 cup margarine
3/4 cup shredded Parmesan cheese
1/2 cup cream
2 tablespoons parsley
Salt and pepper to taste

Cook fettuccine according to directions on package; drain.

Melt margarine in saucepan over medium heat. Slowly stir in cheese and cream until well blended. Stirring constantly, heat the sauce to boiling point. Remove from heat; stir in parsley. Mix with cooked fettuccine and toss. Season with salt and pepper.

Yield: 4 servings

Fettuccine with Wilted Escarole and Mushrooms

3/4 lb. fettuccine
1/4 cup olive oil
4 garlic cloves, thinly sliced
1/2 teaspoon red pepper, crushed
1 1/2 (5 oz.) cup mushrooms, thinly sliced
Salt and pepper to taste
1 (1/2 lb.) head escarole, cored and cut into 1-inch ribbons
6 tablespoons Parmesan cheese (plus more for serving)

Cook pasta according to package directions; drain. Reserve 1 cup of cooking water.

Using a large deep skillet, heat olive oil over medium-high heat. Add garlic and red pepper. Sauté over medium heat 30 seconds, until fragrant but not browned. Add mushrooms and season with salt and pepper. Cook about 5 minutes, until vegetables soften and begin to brown. Add escarole and cook until wilted.

Add pasta along with reserved cooking water and heat until the sauce is slightly thickened, about 2 minutes. Season with salt and pepper as needed. Add Parmesan cheese and toss to coat.

Yield: 4 servings

Pistachio Pasta

1 (8 oz.) penne pasta
2 tablespoons butter
1 large yellow onion, thinly sliced
1/2 cup green bell pepper, diced
1/2 cup red bell pepper, diced
2 tablespoons garlic, minced
1/4 lb. prosciutto, diced
1 cup pistachios, coarsely chopped
1 (2.25) can sliced olives
1 1/2 teaspoons dried rosemary crumbled
1/2 cup extra-virgin olive oil
4 oz. blue cheese, crumbled

Cook pasta according to package directions; drain and set aside.

Melt butter. In a large skillet over medium-high heat, sauté onion until tender. Add peppers, garlic, prosciutto, pistachios, olives, rosemary and olive oil to skillet. Continue cooking, stirring until hot. Add crumbled blue cheese. Toss with pasta and serve.

Yield: 4 to 6 servings

Fettuccine with Gorgonzola

1/2 lb. fresh spinach
1 cup heavy cream
3 oz. Gorgonzola cheese, grated
4 tablespoons butter
1 oz. vodka
Salt and pepper
1/4 lb. reduced fat ricotta cheese, grated
1 lb. fettuccine
3 oz. shredded Parmesan cheese

Wash spinach and shake to remove excess water. Cook spinach in the water clinging to the leaves; drain and chop.

In a saucepan, bring cream to a simmer. Add Gorgonzola cheese, butter and vodka. Blend; add salt and pepper to taste. Add spinach and ricotta; simmer and stir until blended.

Cook noodles according to package directions; drain. Pour sauce over noodles and toss to coat. Sprinkle with Parmesan cheese and toss again. Serve immediately.

Yield: 6 servings.

Linguine and Mushrooms

1/3 cup extra-virgin olive oil
2 tablespoons butter
3/4 lb. linguine
3 cloves garlic, chopped
2 cups mushrooms, sliced
Salt and pepper, to taste
1/8 teaspoon red pepper flakes (optional)
1/2 cup Parmesan or Romano cheese, grated
1/2 cup parsley, chopped

In a medium saucepan, heat olive oil and melt butter over low heat. Meanwhile, cook linguine according to package directions. Add garlic and mushrooms to oil and butter, stirring so garlic doesn't burn. Add salt and pepper, to taste. Add red pepper flakes, if desired. After a few minutes, lower heat.

Drain pasta well, and add to sauce; toss. Sprinkle with grated Parmesan cheese and top with parsley.

Yield: 3 servings

Steak Italiano

8 oz. penne rigate
1 (3/4 lb.) round steak, cut in thin strips
1 (4 oz.) can or jar mushroom pieces, drained
1/2 cup onion, chopped
2 cloves garlic, finely chopped
2 tablespoons extra-virgin olive oil
1 (26 oz.) jar Mushroom Pasta Sauce
1/2 cup dry red wine
1/2 cup water
1 teaspoon beef bouillon granules
Freshly shredded Parmesan cheese

Cook pasta according to package directions; drain and set aside.

In a large skillet, over medium-high heat, cook and stir steak, mushrooms, onion and garlic in olive oil until vegetables are tender and steak is browned. Add pasta sauce, wine, water and bouillon. Bring to a boil; reduce heat. Cover and simmer 20 minutes or until beef is tender. Serve over hot penne rigate; top with Parmesan cheese.

Yield: 8 servings

Black Pepper Fettuccine with Veal, Peas and Cream

1/2 lb. veal scallopini, cut in strips
1 cup flour
2 tablespoons butter
2 shallots, diced
2 tablespoons sweet vermouth
1 egg yolk
2 cups heavy cream
1 cup frozen peas
Salt and pepper to taste
3 lb. fettuccine
1/4 cup Parmesan cheese
1/3 cup mint leaves, julienned

Dredge veal in flour, season with salt and set aside. Heat butter in a large saucepan. Add veal and brown on both sides. Remove veal and reduce heat to medium. Add shallots. Cook until translucent. Remove saucepan from heat. Add vermouth and cook until liquid is reduced by half.

Mix egg yolk with cream and add to saucepan. Simmer, stirring occasionally, until thickened. Add peas, veal; add salt and pepper to taste.

Cook noodles according to package directions; drain. Toss with cream sauce. Add Parmesan cheese and top with mint leaves.

Yield: 4 servings

Macaroni and Garbanzos

1 (16 oz.) pkg. elbow macaroni
1/3 cup olive oil
1 to 2 cloves garlic, minced
1 (16 oz.) can garbanzos chick peas, undrained
1 to 2 tablespoons parsley
Romano or Parmesan cheese

Cook pasta according to package directions; drain.

Heat olive oil in medium skillet. Reduce heat to low, add
garlic and cook until golden brown. Add peas with liquid.
Stir in macaroni, parsley and Romano or Parmesan cheese.

Yield: 4 servings

Quick & Easy Hamburger Casserole

1 lb. lean ground beef
1 medium onion, chopped
1 green bell pepper, chopped
2 cups stewed tomatoes
1 cup elbow macaroni
1 teaspoon salt
1/4 teaspoon black pepper
American cheese slices

Using a large skillet, brown hamburger, onion and bell pepper. Stir in tomatoes, macaroni, salt and pepper. Cover and simmer 30 minutes. Turn off stove. Put cheese slices on top and let stand until melted.

Yield: 4 servings

Baked Pasta

Vermicelli Casserole

1 (16 oz.) pkg. vermicelli
3 cups low fat cottage cheese
3 cups low fat sour cream
2 cloves garlic, crushed
2 onions, minced
1/2 lb. sliced bacon, fried crisp and crumbled
2 tablespoons Worcestershire sauce
Dash liquid hot pepper seasoning
4 tablespoons salt
3 tablespoons horseradish
1/4 cup Parmesan cheese

Cook pasta according to package directions; drain.

In a large bowl, mix cottage cheese, sour cream, garlic, onion, bacon, Worcestershire sauce, hot pepper seasoning, salt and horseradish. Add noodles and toss with 2 forks until well mixed. Turn into deep 3 1/2 quart casserole dish.

Cover and bake for 30 to 40 minutes at 350 degrees. Remove cover and sprinkle with Parmesan cheese. Broil until golden.

Yield: 12 servings

Baked Mostaccioli

12 oz. mostaccioli
1 (24 oz.) jar mushroom pasta sauce
1 cup (4 oz.) reduced fat mozzarella cheese, shredded
1/2 (3.5 oz.) package sliced pepperoni, chopped
1 to 2 tablespoons pepperoncini salad peppers, chopped
1/4 teaspoon black pepper

Cook pasta according to package directions; drain.

In a large bowl, combine hot mostaccioli, pasta sauce, half mozzarella cheese, pepperoni, salad peppers and pepper. Spoon into 2-quart casserole dish; cover.

Bake at 375 degrees F. for 20 minutes. Uncover; sprinkle with remaining cheese. Bake for 5 to 10 minutes until heated through and cheese is bubbly.

Yield: 8 to 12 servings

Macaroni Au Gratin

1 (8 oz.) pkg. elbow macaroni
1 (10.5 oz.) can low fat cream of celery soup
1 cup low fat evaporated milk
1 1/2 cups Cheddar cheese, grated
1 teaspoon Dijon mustard
Salt and pepper
1/4 cup cracker crumbs or breadcrumbs, finely crushed

Cook macaroni according to package directions; drain. Mix
with the rest of the ingredients; pour into baking dish.
Sprinkle cracker crumbs on top and bake at 350 degrees F.
for 30 minutes.

Yield: 4 servings

Ziti with Three Cheeses

1 (16 oz.) pkg. ziti
1 (15 oz.) container low fat ricotta cheese
2 cups reduced fat mozzarella cheese, shredded (divided)
1 egg, lightly beaten
2 tablespoons parsley, finely chopped
1 clove garlic, minced
Salt and pepper to taste
1/2 teaspoon basil
1/4 cup Parmesan cheese
Non-stick cooking spray

Cook ziti according to package directions; drain.

Blend ricotta, 1 cup mozzarella, egg, parsley, garlic, salt, pepper and basil together in a large mixing bowl. Add ziti and mix well. Spray a casserole dish with non-stick cooking spray; pour in ziti mixture. Top with remaining mozzarella and grated Parmesan.

Bake at 350 degrees F. for 30 minutes, until golden.

Yield: 8 servings.

Lasagna Rolls

8 lasagna noodles
1 (10 oz.) pkg. frozen spinach, chopped
1 (15 oz.) carton low fat ricotta cheese
2 tablespoons Parmesan cheese
1/8 teaspoon black pepper
1 (28 oz.) can tomato sauce

Cook noodles according to package directions. Drain.

Prepare spinach according to package directions; drain and squeeze out water. In a medium bowl, combine spinach, ricotta, Parmesan cheese and pepper.

Pour some tomato sauce in a 9x13-inch baking dish. Spread about 1/4 cup of Ricotta filling on each noodle and roll up. Place rolls in baking dish and top with more sauce. Cover and bake 30 to 45 minutes at 375 degrees F.

Yield: 4 servings

Macaroni and Cheese

1 1/2 cups elbow macaroni
4 tablespoons butter plus additional for topping
3 tablespoons flour
2 cups low fat milk
1 (8 oz.) pkg. sharp cheddar cheese, shredded
1/4 to 1/2 cup cracker crumbs

Cook pasta according to package directions; drain.

In medium saucepan, over medium heat, melt butter; add flour and stir for 3 minutes. Add milk and cook until smooth and thick, stirring constantly.

Remove from heat and add cheese. Stir until cheese melts. Combine sauce and macaroni. Pour into a large casserole dish. Sprinkle with cracker crumbs and dot with butter. Bake at 350 degrees F. for 30 minutes.

Yield: 4 servings

Italian Hot Dish

2 cups penne pasta
1/2 lb. bulk Italian sausage
1/2 cup onion, chopped
Green bell pepper, diced small
Salt and pepper
1 (26 oz.) jar spaghetti sauce
2 tablespoons Italian seasoning
1 (4.5 oz.) jar mushrooms, drained
2 cups reduced fat mozzarella cheese, shredded (divided)

Cook pasta according to package directions; rinse and drain.

In a large skillet, brown sausage, onion, bell pepper, salt and pepper. Mix cooked pasta, spaghetti sauce, sausage mixture, Italian seasoning, mushrooms and 1 cup mozzarella.

Ladle mixture into an 8x11-inch baking dish or 2-quart casserole dish. Cover and bake for 40 minutes at 350 degrees F. Uncover; layer 1 cup mozzarella on top and bake uncovered 8 to 10 minutes longer.

Yield: 2 to 3 servings

Spicy Ziti

1 lb. ziti or penne pasta
2 tablespoons olive oil
1 lb. bulk Italian sausage
3 or 4 tablespoons onion, chopped
1 teaspoon garlic, minced
1 (28 oz.) can tomato sauce
1 1/2 teaspoons crushed red pepper
1 (14.5 oz.) can low-sodium chicken broth
8 oz. Havarti cheese with jalapeno
1 1/2 cups Parmesan cheese, shredded
2 (8 oz.) cartons heavy whipping cream
Salt and pepper to taste

Cook pasta according to package directions; drain and toss with 2 tablespoons olive oil.

In a large skillet, cook sausage; drain grease. Add onion and garlic to skillet; cook until onion is transparent. Mix in tomato sauce and red pepper; bring to a boil. Add chicken broth; return to boil. Simmer 30 minutes. Remove from heat; Blend in both cheeses; add cream when cheese melts. Salt and pepper to taste.

Mix pasta with sauce and place in a 9x13-inch baking dish. Bake at 350 degrees F. for 30 minutes, covered with foil. After 30 minutes, remove foil and bake additional 30 minutes. This is spicy. Reduce crushed red pepper if desired.

Yield: 4 servings

Baked Penne and Smoked Sausage

8 oz. penne pasta
1(16 oz.) pkg. smoked sausage, cut in 1/4 inch slices
1 (10.75 oz.) can low fat cream of celery soup
1 1/2 cups low fat milk
1 cup frozen peas
1 cup reduced fat mozzarella cheese, shredded (divided)
1 1/2 cups Cheddar French fried onions (divided)

Cook pasta according to package directions; drain.

Brown smoked sausage; drain. In a medium bowl, combine soup with milk. Combine pasta, peas, sausage, 1/2 cup mozzarella cheese and 1/2 cup French fried onions in a 3-quart baking dish. Bake at 375 degrees F. for 30 minutes or until hot. Top with remaining onions, cheese and broil until topping is golden.

Yield: 4 servings

Macaroni Bake

1 1/2 cups elbow macaroni
2 eggs, beaten
1 cup milk
Salt and pepper to taste
1 lb. lean ground beef
1/2 teaspoon oregano
1 (8 oz.) can tomato sauce
1 cup cheddar cheese, grated
Non-stick cooking spray

Cook pasta according to package directions; drain. Stir in eggs, milk, salt and pepper. Spray a 9x13-inch baking dish with non-stick cooking spray. Bake for 10 minutes at 400 degrees F. Remove from oven and set aside.

Brown meat and drain. Mix in oregano, tomato sauce and cheese. Spread meat mixture on top of macaroni. Bake at 350 degrees F. for 15 minutes or until cheese melts.

Yield: 2 servings

Pepperoni Casserole

1 (12 oz.) pkg. rigatoni
3 tablespoons olive oil
2 lb. lean ground beef
1 1/2 lb. pkg. pepperoni
2 cups celery, chopped
2 cups onion, chopped
2 cups green bell pepper, chopped
1 cup hot water
1 qt. (32 oz.) spaghetti sauce
1 (10.75 oz.) can tomato soup
1 (4 oz.) can mushrooms and juice, sliced
1 cup black olives, sliced
1/2 lb. reduced fat mozzarella cheese, shredded

Cook the rigatoni according to package directions; drain.

Brown meat in oil until no longer pink; add pepperoni, celery, onion, bell pepper and cook until vegetables soften. Add water, spaghetti sauce, tomato soup, mushrooms, olives and rigatoni to meat mixture.

Spread in baking dish and bake at 350 degrees F. for 35 minutes. Sprinkle with cheese and continue to bake until cheese is melted.

Yield: 4 servings

Spicy Rigatoni Bake

1 (16 oz.) pkg. rigatoni
1 lb. lean ground beef
1 medium onion, chopped
1 (28 oz.) can tomato puree
2 (8 oz. each) cans tomato sauce
1/2 cup ripe olives, sliced
1/4 cup Parmesan cheese
1 teaspoon seasoned salt
1 teaspoon dried oregano
1/2 teaspoon crushed red pepper
2 tablespoons margarine or butter
1 cup reduced fat mozzarella cheese, shredded

In a large skillet, cook ground beef and onion until beef is browned; drain. Stir in tomato puree, tomato sauce, olives, Parmesan cheese, seasoned salt, oregano and crushed red pepper. Bring to a boil. Reduce heat; simmer 15 minutes.

Prepare pasta according to package directions; drain. Add margarine and toss to coat.

Spread rigatoni in a 3-quart casserole dish; cover with hot meat sauce. Top evenly with mozzarella cheese. Broil until cheese melts, about 2 to 3 minutes.

Yield: 4 servings

Italian Casserole

1 (16 oz.) pkg. rigatoni
1 lb. bulk hot Italian sausage
1 lb. lean ground beef
1 large onion, chopped
1 (4 oz.) can mushrooms, drained
2 cups (1 /2 lb.) extra-sharp Cheddar cheese, shredded
3 cups reduced fat mozzarella cheese, shredded (divided)
2 (15 oz. each) cans pizza sauce
1 teaspoon garlic powder
2 tablespoons Italian seasoning

Brown sausage, ground beef and onions; add mushrooms. In a large bowl, combine meat mixture, Cheddar cheese, 1 cup mozzarella cheese, pizza sauce, garlic powder and Italian seasoning.

Cook pasta according to directions on package; drain. Mix noodles with meat mixture and pour into a large casserole dish.

Bake at 375 degrees for 30 minutes. Remove from oven, top with reserved mozzarella cheese and bake an additional 15 minutes.

May be refrigerated overnight before baking.

Yield: 4 servings

Crockpot Macaroni and Cheese

1 1/2 to 2 cups elbow macaroni
2 tablespoons olive oil
1 (13 oz.) can low fat evaporated skim milk
1 teaspoon salt
3 cups sharp processed cheese, shredded
1 1/2 cups 2% milk
1/4 cup butter melted
2 tablespoons onion, minced (optional)
Non-stick cooking spray

Cook pasta according to directions on package; drain.

Toss cooked macaroni in oil. Add evaporated milk, salt, cheese, milk, butter and onion. Lightly spray slow cooker with non-stick cooking spray. Place mixture in slow cooker and stir. Cook 3 to 4 hours on Low.

Yield: 4 servings

Grandma's Scalloped Corn

3/4 cup low fat milk
2 tablespoons Cheese Whiz
1 (14.75 oz.) can cream style corn
1 (15 oz.) can whole kernel corn, drained
3/4 cup elbow macaroni, uncooked
Butter
Non-stick cooking spray

Warm milk and add Cheese Whiz; stir until cheese melts.
Add corn and uncooked macaroni. Spray a casserole dish
with non-stick cooking spray. Pour macaroni mixture into
casserole dish. Dot the top with butter and bake at 350
degrees F. for one hour.

Quick-cook method:

Cook pasta according to package directions; drain.
Eliminate milk. Mix all ingredients in a heavy saucepan and
heat until cheese is dissolved. Bake at 350 degrees F. for 30
minutes until bubbly hot and golden brown.

Yield: 3 to 4 servings

Macaroni Hamburger Casserole

2 cups macaroni
2 lb. lean ground beef
1 small onion, chopped
2 (10.5 oz. each) cans low fat cream of chicken soup
1/2 cup low fat milk
8 oz. Cheddar cheese, shredded

Cook ground beef and onions together; drain fat. Blend in cream of chicken soup, uncooked macaroni, milk and cheese. Place in a 9x13-inch baking dish coated with non-stick cooking spray. Bake 45 minutes at 350 degrees F.

Yield: 4 servings

Lazy Lasagna

1 (16 oz.) pkg. lasagna noodles
1 lb. lean ground beef
1 lb. bulk Italian sausage
1 teaspoon minced onion
1 teaspoon garlic powder
1 (6 oz.) can tomato paste
1 (8 oz.) can tomato sauce
1 1/2 cups water
1/2 teaspoon salt
1/2 teaspoon black pepper
1 teaspoon chili powder
1 teaspoon oregano
1 teaspoon basil leaves
1 teaspoon granulated sugar
1/2 cup Parmesan cheese
4 cups reduced fat mozzarella cheese, shredded

Cook ground beef and sausage, onion and garlic powder; drain off fat. In a medium bowl, combine tomato paste, tomato sauce, water, salt, pepper, chili powder, oregano, basil and sugar; add to meat mixture. Simmer for 1 hour, stirring frequently. This is a thin mixture.

Layer in the following order: 1/3 of - meat mixture, 1/2 of - Parmesan cheese (sprinkled over mixture), uncooked noodles and mozzarella cheese. Repeat layers, ending with meat sauce. Cover with aluminum foil and bake at 350 degrees F. for 45 minutes to 1 hour.

Yield: 6 servings

Lasagna Cordon Blue

8 oz. lasagna noodles
1/4 cup butter
1/3 cup flour
1/8 teaspoon garlic powder
1 tablespoon dried onion
1/8 teaspoon black pepper
1 cup low fat milk
2 cups low-sodium chicken broth
1 cup Parmesan cheese
1 (3 oz.) can mushrooms, drained
1 (10 oz.) pkg. frozen cut asparagus (or broccoli or green beans)
2 cups cooked chicken or turkey
1 (5 oz.) pkg. sliced or reduced fat mozzarella cheese, shredded
1 (6 oz.) pkg. thinly sliced ham

Cook noodles according to package directions; drain.

Melt butter in saucepan; blend in flour, garlic powder, onion and pepper. Add milk and chicken broth; stir and cook until bubbly. Stir in 1/2 cup Parmesan cheese and mushrooms.

In a 9x13-inch baking dish, layer 1/2 the noodles, asparagus, chicken or turkey, mozzarella cheese, 1/3 milk mixture, ham, remaining noodles, and then remaining milk mixture. Sprinkle with remaining 1/2 cup Parmesan cheese.

Bake at 350 degrees F. for 35 minutes. Let stand 10 minutes before cutting.

Yield: 6 servings

Mushroom Lasagna

1 lb. lasagna
1 lb. fresh mushrooms
4 tablespoons olive oil
1 cup onion, chopped
4 cups tomato sauce
1/4 teaspoon basil
1 teaspoon oregano
1 cup low fat cottage cheese
3/4 lb. reduced fat mozzarella cheese, shredded
5 tablespoons Parmesan cheese
Non-stick cooking spray

Cook noodles according to package directions; drain.

Sauté sliced mushrooms in olive oil. Add onion and cook until onions are soft and transparent. Add tomato sauce, basil, oregano; simmer.

Spray a 9x13-inch baking dish with non-stick cooking spray. Place a layer of noodles in the baking dish (1/3 of the noodles). Layer with 1/3 of the sauce, 1/2 of the cottage cheese and 1/2 of the mozzarella. Repeat, ending with a layer of lasagna and sauce.

Add Parmesan cheese on top and bake at 400 degrees F. for 45 minutes.

Yield: 8 servings

Lasagna Florentine

16 lasagna noodles
2 tablespoons olive oil
8 oz. mushrooms, sliced
3 medium carrots, finely chopped
1 medium onion, finely chopped
2 cloves garlic, finely chopped
1 (24 oz.) jar roasted garlic pasta sauce
2 eggs, beaten or 1/2 cup egg beaters
1 (10 oz.) pkg. frozen chopped broccoli, thawed and squeezed dry
1 (9 oz.) pkg. frozen chopped spinach, thawed and squeezed dry
15 oz. fat free ricotta cheese or fat free cottage cheese
2 cups reduced fat mozzarella, shredded
1/4 cup Parmesan cheese
1 teaspoon Italian seasoning
1 teaspoon salt

Cook noodles according to package directions; drain.

In a 12-inch skillet, heat olive oil over medium heat and cook mushrooms, carrots, onion and garlic until carrots are almost tender, about 5 minutes. Add pasta sauce and heat.

In a medium bowl, combine eggs, broccoli, spinach, all 3 cheeses, Italian seasoning and salt; set aside.

Spread 1/2 cup sauce mixture in a 13x9-inch baking dish. Arrange 4 noodles over sauce, overlapping edges slightly. Spread 1/3 of the cheese mixture over noodles. Repeat layers ending with noodles. Add remaining sauce and 1/2 cup mozzarella cheese to top.

Cover with foil and bake at 375 degrees F. for 40 minutes. Remove foil and continue baking 10 minutes or until bubbling. Let stand 10 minutes before serving.

Yield: 8 servings

Baked Spaghetti with Mushroom Soup

12 oz. spaghetti
1 lb. lean ground beef
1 cup onion, chopped
1 cup green bell pepper, diced
1 tablespoon margarine
1 (28 oz.) can tomatoes with liquid, cut up
1 (4 oz.) can mushrooms, drained
1 (2.25 oz.) sliced ripe olives, drained
2 teaspoons dried oregano
2 cups cheddar cheese, shredded
1 (10.5) can low fat mushroom soup
1/4 cup water
1/4 cup Parmesan cheese

Cook spaghetti according to package directions; drain.

In a large skillet, brown and drain ground beef. Remove from skillet, then sauté onion and green bell pepper in margarine until translucent. Add tomatoes, mushrooms, olives and season with oregano. Mix in ground beef and simmer, uncovered, for 10 minutes.

Prepare a 9x13-inch baking dish with non-stick cooking spray and place 1/2 of the pasta in the bottom of the dish. Layer with 1/2 of the vegetable/beef mixture and 1 cup of shredded cheddar cheese. Repeat layers.

Combine soup and water; pour over the layers. Add Parmesan cheese to the top and bake, uncovered for about 35 minutes at 350 degrees F.

Yield: 4 servings

Pirogies

2 cups dry cottage cheese or cheese curds
1 egg
1 teaspoon onion salt, divided
1 cup (4 oz.) cheddar cheese, shredded
2 cups mashed potatoes
Salt and pepper to taste
9 lasagna noodles
1 cup chopped onion
3/4 cup margarine or butter

Combine cottage cheese, egg and half the onion salt in a medium bowl.

In a separate bowl, combine cheddar cheese, mashed potatoes, salt, pepper and remaining 1/2 teaspoon onion salt.

Cook noodles according to package directions; drain. Layer 3 noodles in a 9x13-inch baking dish. Layer cottage cheese mixture, 3 noodles, potato mixture and remaining 3 noodles over the first layer.

Sauté onion in margarine to soften and spread over top of casserole. Bake, uncovered, at 350 degrees F. for 30 minutes.

Yield: 8 servings

Macaroni Loaf

3/4 cup elbow macaroni
1 1/2 cups milk, scalded
3 egg yolks, beaten
1 cup soft bread crumbs
1/4 cup butter
1 pimento, chopped
3 egg whites, beaten stiff
1 tablespoon parsley, chopped
1 teaspoon onion, chopped
1 teaspoon salt
1/2 cup cheddar cheese, grated

Cook pasta according to directions on package; rinse and drain.

In a large bowl, combine all ingredients; bake in a loaf pan placed in a pan of hot water. Bake at 350 degrees F. for 35 minutes, or until firm.

Yield: 2 servings

Easy Spaghetti Pie

Sauce:

1 lb. lean hamburger
1/2 cup onion, diced
1 (15.5 oz.) jar spaghetti sauce

Pie shell:

8 oz. pkg. spaghetti
2 tablespoons butter or margarine
1/3 cup Parmesan cheese, grated
2 eggs, lightly beaten

Filling:

1 cup reduced fat cottage cheese
1 cup reduced fat shredded mozzarella cheese

Brown onion with hamburger and drain. Add spaghetti sauce; simmer for 5 minutes.

Cook spaghetti according to package directions; drain. Stir butter or margarine, grated Parmesan cheese and eggs into freshly cooked spaghetti.

Spray a 10-inch pie plate with nonstick spray; line with spaghetti mixture to form a crust. Pour a thin layer of sauce over noodles. Spread reduced fat cottage cheese over bottom of crust and cover with remaining sauce. Bake at 350 degrees F. for 30 minutes. Cover with mozzarella cheese and place in oven to melt. Let stand before serving. Yield: 4 to 6 servings.

Macaroni Pizza

2 cups elbow macaroni
1/2 cup low fat milk
1 egg, beaten
1/2 teaspoon salt
1 1/2 cups spaghetti sauce
1 (10 oz.) can diced tomatoes and green chilies, drained
1 (5 oz.) pkg. pepperoni, sliced
1 onion, chopped
1 green bell pepper, chopped
1 (4 oz.) can sliced mushrooms, drained
1 cup sliced ripe olives
1 teaspoon Italian seasoning
2 cups reduced fat mozzarella cheese, shredded
Non-stick cooking spray

Cook macaroni according to package directions; drain.

In a large bowl, blend milk, egg and salt; add macaroni and mix. Spread on a 10x15-inch baking sheet sprayed with non-stick cooking spray. Combine spaghetti sauce with tomatoes and green chilies. Ladle over macaroni.

Top with pepperoni, onion, bell pepper, mushrooms, ripe olives, Italian seasoning and mozzarella cheese. Bake at 350 degrees F. until hot macaroni is set (about 30 minutes). Let stand 5 minutes before cutting.

Yield: 4 to 6 servings

Crunchy Ham Casserole

2 cups elbow macaroni
1 1/2 cups cooked ham, cubed
1 (10.5 oz.) can low fat cream of chicken soup
1/2 cup low fat sour cream
1/2 cup milk
1 (10 oz.) pkg. frozen broccoli spears, cooked and drained
1 cup cheddar cheese, shredded
1 cup French fried onions

Cook pasta according to package directions; drain.

Spray a 9x13-inch baking dish with non-stick cooking spray. In the baking dish, combine macaroni and ham.

In a bowl, blend soup, sour cream and milk; pour half the soup mixture over macaroni. Place broccoli on top. Pour remaining soup mixture on top and sprinkle with cheese.

Bake uncovered at 350 degrees F. for 20 minutes. Cover with French fried onions and bake an additional 5 minutes.

Yield: 4 servings

Stuffed Pasta

Ham-Stuffed Manicotti with Cheese Sauce

1/4 lb. manicotti (8 shells)
1/4 cup onion, chopped
2 tablespoons olive oil
1/4 lb. mushrooms, sliced
3 cups (1/2 lb.) ground cooked ham
3 tablespoons Parmesan cheese, freshly grated
1/4 cup green bell pepper, chopped
3 tablespoons butter
3 tablespoons flour
2 cups low fat milk
1 (4 oz.) cup grated Swiss cheese
Non-stick cooking spray

Cook pasta according to package directions; drain, rinse with cold water and drain again. Set aside.

In a large skillet, sauté onion in oil until soft, about 5 minutes. Add mushrooms and cook additional 3 to 4 minutes. Remove from heat and add cooked ham. Set aside until cool; stir in Parmesan cheese.

Sauté bell pepper in butter until soft, 3 to 4 minutes. At a moderate heat and stirring constantly, blend in flour and cook until mix is smooth. Add milk, stirring constantly until sauce thickens. Add Swiss cheese and stir to blend.

Stuff manicotti with cooled ham mixture. Place stuffed shells in 9x13-inch baking dish sprayed with non-stick cooking spray. Pour sauce over all. Bake at 350 degrees F. for 30 to 40 minutes, until bubbling and lightly browned.
Yield: 4 servings

Tortellini and Spinach Pasta

1 19 oz. pkg. frozen cheese-filled tortellini
2 tablespoons olive oil
1/2 cup onion, chopped
3 cloves garlic, minced
1 (9 oz.) pkg. frozen spinach, thawed and drained
1 cup tomato, seeded and cubed
1/4 cup fresh basil
1/4 teaspoon salt
1/8 teaspoon black pepper
1 cup whipping cream
1/4 cup Parmesan cheese

Cook pasta according to directions on package; drain and cover to keep warm.

In a large skillet, sauté onion and garlic in olive oil. Add spinach, tomato, basil, salt and pepper. Cook 5 minutes, stirring occasionally. Stir in whipping cream and cheese; cook until cheese melts. Stir in tortellini and heat.

Yield: 4 servings

Ravioli

To make 3/4 lb. of noodles:

1 to 1 1/2 cups flour
1 egg
1 egg white
1 tablespoon olive oil
1 teaspoon salt
Few drops of water

Pour flour in large mixing bowl or in a heap on pastry board. Make well in center; add egg, egg white, oil and salt. Mix together with a fork or fingers until dough can be gathered into a rough ball. Moisten any remaining dry bits of flour with drops of water and press into the ball.

Divide dough into 4 pieces and roll out first 1/4 of dough as thin as possible. Cover rolled pasta with damp towel to prevent drying out. Roll out second 1/4 of dough to same size and shape. Place a mound of 1 tablespoon cheese or meat mixture every 2 inches across and down the pasta. Dip pastry brush or index finger in water. Make vertical and horizontal lines between the mounds of ravioli filling. Use enough water to wet lines evenly as water acts as bond to hold finished ravioli together.

Carefully spread second sheet of rolled out pasta on top of first one, pressing down firmly around filling and along wetted lines. Using a ravioli cutter, pastry wheel or small knife, cut the pasta into squares along the lines. Separate mounds and set them aside on wax paper.

Roll out other two portions of dough in same fashion. To cook, drop ravioli into 6 to 8 quarts rapidly boiling salted water and stir gently with wooden spoon to keep pasta from sticking to one another or to go to the bottom of pot. Boil for about 8 minutes until tender. Drain thoroughly in large sieve. Serve with favorite tomato sauce or add butter and freshly grated Romano cheese and gently stir all together immediately before serving.

Cheese Filling:

1 1/2 lb. Ricotta cheese
3/4 cup grated Romano cheese
2 teaspoons grated onion
3 egg yolks
1 1/2 teaspoons salt

In a large mixing bowl, combine Ricotta cheese, Romano cheese, onion, egg yolks and salt. Carefully stir together until well mixed. Set aside until dough is rolled out.

Meat Filling:

3 tablespoons butter
4 tablespoons onion, chopped
1 lb. ground beef
1 (10 oz.) frozen package or 3/4 lb. fresh spinach, cooked, squeezed and chopped
1/2 cup grated Romano cheese
1/8 teaspoon of ground nutmeg
3 eggs
Salt to taste

Melt butter in a small skillet and cook onions, stirring often for 8 minutes or until transparent but not brown. Add ground beef and cook, stirring constantly, until meat loses redness and liquid in pan cooks away. Transfer to a large mixing bowl and stir in chopped spinach, cheese and nutmeg. Beat eggs lightly and add to meat mixture, taste and season with salt.

Cannelloni

Filling:
1 (10 oz.) package frozen spinach, chopped, thawed
1 tablespoon vegetable oil
1/2 cup onion, finely chopped
2 cloves garlic, minced
1 lb. lean ground beef
1 egg
2 tablespoons Parmesan cheese, grated
1 teaspoon dried Italian seasoning, divided
1/4 teaspoon salt
1/8 teaspoon pepper

Sauce:
2 cups tomato sauce
1/8 teaspoon salt
1/4 teaspoon Italian seasoning
1/4 cup Parmesan cheese, grated

12 manicotti shells

Cook pasta according to package directions; drain and set aside.

Filling: Place spinach between paper towels and squeeze until spinach is barely moist. Coat a large skillet with vegetable oil; place over medium heat until hot. Add onion and garlic; sauté for 2 minutes. Add spinach; sauté for 1 minute. Place mixture in a large bowl; set aside. Cook ground beef in skillet over medium heat until browned, stirring occasionally. Drain well and add to spinach mixture. Add egg, cheese, Italian seasoning, salt and pepper; stir well and set aside.

Sauce: Combine tomato sauce, salt and Italian seasoning in a bowl. Spread 1 cup of tomato sauce mixture over bottom of 13x9x2-inch baking dish. Stuff each shell with 1/3 cup spinach mixture and arrange on top of tomato sauce. Top with the remaining tomato sauce and 1/4 cup Parmesan cheese. Cover and bake at 375 degrees F. for 30 minutes or until thoroughly heated.

Yield: 8 servings.

Tortellini Bake

1 (10 oz.) pkg. fresh refrigerated cheese tortellini
1 tablespoon olive oil
1 small zucchini, diced
1 yellow squash, diced
1 onion, diced
1 red bell pepper, diced
1 teaspoon dried basil
1/4 teaspoon salt
1/8 teaspoon black pepper
1 cup reduced-fat mozzarella cheese, shredded
1 cup light cream

Cook pasta according to directions on package; drain and rinse in hot water.

Heat oil in a medium saucepan; cook zucchini, yellow squash, onion, bell pepper, basil, salt and pepper until vegetables are tender crisp.

Combine tortellini with vegetable mixture, mozzarella and cream in a 1 1/2-quart baking dish. Bake uncovered at 375 degrees F. for 20 minutes or until heated through.

Yield: 6 to 8 servings

Manicotti with Cheese Filling

1 (8 oz.) package manicotti
2 cups mozzarella cheese, shredded
2 cups (15 oz.) ricotta cheese
1/4 cup Parmesan cheese, grated
2 tablespoons parsley, chopped
1/2 teaspoon salt
1/4 teaspoon pepper
1 (32 oz.) jar spaghetti sauce

Cook pasta according to package directions; drain and set aside. Cool in a single layer on parchment paper, aluminum foil or baking sheets to prevent manicotti from sticking together.

In a large bowl, combine mozzarella cheese, ricotta cheese, Parmesan cheese, parsley, salt and pepper. Spoon cheese filling mixture into manicotti.

Spread a thin layer of sauce on bottom of a 13x9x2-inch baking dish. Arrange manicotti in single layer over sauce. Cover with remaining sauce. Cover dish with aluminum foil. Bake at 350 degrees F. for about 40 minutes. Remove foil; baking 15 minutes longer.

Yield: 6 to 8 servings

Stuffed Jumbo Shells

24 jumbo pasta shells
8 oz. low fat Ricotta cheese
8 oz. low fat cottage cheese
16 oz. reduced fat mozzarella, shredded
1 tablespoon parsley flakes
1 teaspoon salt
1/4 teaspoon black pepper
1/2 lb. Italian sausage or lean ground beef
1 (32 oz.) jar spaghetti sauce
1/4 cup additional mozzarella cheese

Cook shells according to package directions; drain.

In a medium bowl, mix Ricotta, cottage cheese, mozzarella, parsley, salt and pepper. Stuff each shell with cheese mixture. Place in 9x13-inch baking dish.

Cook meat; drain. Combine spaghetti sauce and meat. Pour over shells. Sprinkle mozzarella on top (1/4 cup). Bake at 350 degrees F. for 30 minutes.

Yield: 4 servings

Pasta with Poultry

Chicken with Sun Dried Tomatoes

1 (16 oz.) pkg. angel hair pasta
4 chicken breasts, cut into bite-sized pieces
2 tablespoons butter
1 1/2 cups mushrooms
1 or 2 cloves garlic, minced
1/3 cup sun-dried tomatoes, chopped
1/2 teaspoons crushed red pepper
1 cup heavy cream
1 cup low-sodium chicken broth
1/3 cup green onion, chopped
1/3 cup cilantro, chopped

Cook pasta according to package directions; drain.

In a large skillet, sauté chicken breast pieces in butter. Add mushrooms, garlic, tomatoes and red pepper. Sauté for an additional 3 minutes. Add cream and chicken broth; cook for 5 to 7 minutes. Add green onions and cilantro to chicken mixture. Pour chicken mixture over pasta and serve.

Yield: 4 servings

Angel Hair Pasta Chicken Lo Mein

1 tablespoon olive oil
2 boneless, skinless chicken breast halves, cut into bite-sized strips
1 garlic clove, minced
1/2 cup water
1/4 teaspoon ginger
1 (10.5 oz.) can low-sodium chicken broth
2 tablespoons soy sauce
4 oz. angel hair pasta, uncooked, broken into thirds
1 (12 oz.) pkg. frozen broccoli, carrots and water chestnuts

Heat olive oil in a large skillet over medium-high heat until hot. Add chicken and garlic; cook until chicken is no longer pink inside. Add water, ginger, chicken broth and soy sauce. Bring to a boil.

Stir in pasta. Stir in frozen vegetables. Return to a boil. Reduce heat to medium-low. Cover and simmer for 5 to 8 minutes or until vegetables and pasta are tender, stirring occasionally.

Yield: 4 servings

Chicken Marinara

1 (16 oz.) pkg. angel hair pasta
4 boneless, skinless chicken breasts
3 cloves garlic, minced
2 cups fresh mushrooms, sliced
1/2 teaspoon Italian seasoning
1 teaspoon dried basil
1/2 cup chicken broth
1 (28 oz.) jar meatless spaghetti sauce
Non-stick cooking spray

Cook pasta according to package directions; drain.

Spray a large skillet with non-stick cooking spray. Add chicken to skillet; cook chicken for 6 minutes per side; remove from skillet and keep warm.

Add garlic, mushrooms, Italian seasoning and basil to skillet. Sauté until mushrooms are tender. Add chicken broth and spaghetti sauce. Add chicken; cover and simmer 10 minutes or until heated through. Serve over hot, cooked pasta.

Yield: 4 servings

Turkey Tetrazzini

1 lb. box linguine
6 tablespoons butter
6 tablespoons flour
3 cups low-sodium chicken broth
1/2 teaspoon salt
1/4 teaspoon black pepper
1/8 teaspoon cayenne pepper
1 cup whipping cream
4 cups cooked turkey, cubed
1 cup fresh mushrooms, sliced
1 (4 oz.) jar pimientos, diced
1/4 cup fresh parsley, chopped
4 or 5 drops hot pepper sauce
1/3 cup Parmesan cheese
Non-stick cooking spray

Cook pasta according to package directions; drain.

Heat butter in a medium saucepan on low heat. Blend in
flour to make a roux. Constantly mixing, add broth, salt,
pepper and cayenne pepper; raise heat to medium-high and
bring to a boil, stirring constantly. Cook until thickened.
Remove from heat; add cream.

Spray a 9x13-inch baking dish with non-stick cooking spray.
Toss 2 cups sauce with linguine; pour into baking dish.
Make a "well" in the center of the noodles, making a 4x6-
inch center area.

Mix turkey, mushrooms, pimientos, parsley and hot pepper
sauce with remaining sauce. Ladle into linguine "well." Top
with Parmesan cheese and bake, covered, at 350 degrees F.
for 30 minutes. Uncover and bake 20 to 30 minutes more, or
it bubbles. Yield: 4 servings

Chicken Casserole Supreme

1 (7 oz.) box elbow macaroni
2 to 3 lb. fryer chicken
1 green bell pepper, chopped
1 tablespoon butter
4 hard-boiled eggs, diced
1 (2 oz.) can pimentos
1 large onion, chopped
1/2 lb. grated American cheese
2 (10.5 oz. each) cans low fat cream of mushroom soup
1 cup chicken broth
1 cup low fat milk
Salt and pepper to taste

Cook pasta according to directions on package; drain.

Cook chicken and remove meat from bones. Sauté bell pepper in butter until soft; set aside.

Mix chicken with macaroni, eggs, pimentos, onion, cheese, sautéed bell pepper, mushroom soup, chicken broth and milk. Salt and pepper to taste. Place in a 9x13-inch baking dish coated with non-stick spray.

Refrigerate overnight. Allow to come to room temperature for 1/2 hour before putting in oven. Bake at 350 degrees F. for 1-1/2 hours or until top is browned.

Yield: 10 to 14 servings

Rotel Chicken

1 (10 oz.) pkg. spaghetti
1 large green bell pepper, chopped
2 large onions, chopped
1/4 cup margarine
4 to 6 skinless chicken breasts
1 (14.5 oz.) can diced Rotel tomatoes
1 lb. Velveeta cheese
1 (8 oz.) can tiny peas or 1 cup chopped broccoli
2/3 cup fresh mushrooms, sliced
Salt and pepper to taste

Cook spaghetti according to package directions; drain.

Sauté bell pepper and onion in margarine; add to spaghetti.
Cut up chicken, cook and season. Add to spaghetti.

Mix Rotel tomatoes, cheese, peas or broccoli and
mushrooms; add to pasta mix, stirring until cheese is
melted. Season to taste with pepper and salt. Divide
between two large casserole dishes and bake at 350
degrees F. for 15 to 20 minutes.

Yield: 6 servings

Chicken-Spaghetti Casserole

8 oz. spaghetti
1 (8 oz.) carton reduced fat ricotta cheese
1 cup (4 oz.) reduced fat shredded mozzarella cheese,
divided
2 tablespoons grated Parmesan cheese
1/2 teaspoon garlic powder
1/2 teaspoon Italian seasoning
1 (26 oz.) jar spaghetti sauce, meatless
1 (14.5 oz.) can Italian diced tomatoes, undrained
1 (4.4 oz.) jar sliced mushrooms, drained
4 chicken patties
Non-stick cooking spray

Cook spaghetti according to package directions; drain.

Combine ricotta, 1/2 of the mozzarella cheese, Parmesan
cheese, garlic powder and Italian seasoning in a small bowl.
In another bowl, combine spaghetti sauce with tomatoes
and mushrooms.

Spray a 9x13-inch baking dish with non-stick cooking spray.
Mix 2 cups sauce with spaghetti and toss to coat. Transfer to
baking dish and top with cheese mixture.

Arrange chicken on cheese and pour remaining spaghetti
sauce on top. Sprinkle with remaining mozzarella. Bake
uncovered at 350 degrees F. for 40 minutes.

Yield: 4 servings

20-Minute Stovetop Chicken Parmesan

4 cups spaghetti
4 boneless, skinless chicken breasts
1 egg, slightly beaten
1/2 cup seasoned bread crumbs
2 tablespoons butter or margarine
2 cups spaghetti sauce
1/2 cup reduced fat mozzarella cheese, shredded
1 tablespoon Parmesan cheese
1 teaspoon parsley flakes

Cook spaghetti according to package directions; drain.

Evenly flatten chicken with a meat mallet. Dip chicken in egg and coat with crumbs. Using a large skillet, over medium heat, melt butter and brown chicken on both sides.

Add spaghetti sauce to chicken. Reduce heat to simmer. Cover and cook 10 minutes. Add mozzarella cheese, Parmesan cheese and parsley on top. Cover and cook until cheese melts. Serve over pasta.

Yield: 4 servings

Easy Chicken Casserole

2 cups cooked chicken or turkey, diced
2 cups elbow macaroni, uncooked
2 (10.5 oz. each) cans low fat mushroom soup
10 oz. low fat milk
1 1/2 cups low-sodium chicken broth
1 small onion, finely chopped
1/2 green bell pepper, finely chopped
Pimiento (optional)
1 (15 oz.) can water chestnuts, sliced
1/2 lb. cheese, grated
1/2 teaspoon salt
Non-stick cooking spray

In a large bowl, combine all ingredients together in order given. Mix well.

Spray a 9x13-inch baking dish with non-stick cooking spray. Add casserole to baking dish; bake at 350 degrees F. for 1 hour.

Yield: 4 servings

Fish and Seafood with Pasta

Buttery Pasta with Shrimp

3 cups vermicelli
3/4 cup butter
1/2 cup onion, chopped
2 (12 oz. each) pkg. frozen cocktail size shrimp, thawed and drained
1 1/2 teaspoons garlic powder
1/2 teaspoon salt
1/2 teaspoon oregano
1/4 teaspoon black pepper
2 cups tomatoes, cubed
Grated Parmesan cheese

Cook pasta according to package directions; drain and set aside.

In a heavy 3-quart saucepan, melt butter over medium heat. Add vermicelli, onion, shrimp, garlic powder, salt, oregano and pepper; stir to blend. Continue cooking over medium heat; stir occasionally until vermicelli is heated through, about 3 to 5 minutes.

Remove from the heat; add tomatoes. Cover and let stand (1 minute or until tomatoes are heated through). Sprinkle with Parmesan cheese and serve.

Yield: 6 servings

Broccoli-Shrimp Sauce for Pasta

6 oz. fettuccine
1/2 lb. (1-1/4 cups) fresh broccoli florets
1 tablespoon butter
3 scallions, sliced
1 clove garlic, minced
1/2 lb. medium shrimp, peeled and deveined
3/4 lb. low fat ricotta cheese
1/4 cup vermouth
Salt and pepper to taste

Cook noodles according to package directions; drain.

Steam broccoli until tender-crisp and drain. Sauté scallions
and garlic in butter in a heavy saucepan for about 2 minutes.
Add shrimp; sauté 2 minutes. Add cheese and vermouth;
mix and heat through, about 2 minutes. Spoon sauce over
warm pasta. Toss with broccoli. Season with salt and
pepper.

Yield: 3 to 4 servings

Cold Fettuccine with Shrimp

3/4 lb. fettuccine
1 lb. medium shrimp, cooked, shelled, and deveined
1/2 cup walnut pieces
1/3 to 1/2 cup lemon juice
1/4 cup vegetable oil
1 tablespoon red wine vinegar
2 tablespoons chopped fresh basil or 2 teaspoons dried
Salt and black pepper to taste

Cook noodles according to package directions; drain.
Combine fettuccine, shrimp and walnuts in a large bowl.

In a small bowl, combine lemon juice, oil, vinegar, basil;
whisk to blend. Pour the lemon dressing over the shrimp
and pasta; toss to mix. Season to taste with salt and pepper.
Serve at cool room temperature.

Yield: 6 to 8 servings

Imitation Crab and Artichoke Casserole

4 tablespoons margarine
1/4 cup flour
2 green onions, chopped
3 1/4 cups milk
1 1/4 cups macaroni
2 cups imitation crabmeat, shredded
1/3 cup sherry
1 (8 oz.) can artichoke hearts, drained
1 cup fresh mushrooms, sliced
1/4 cup Parmesan cheese, grated
Paprika

Melt margarine in a saucepan; add flour and stir until smooth. Add onions. Stirring constantly, slowly add milk. Continuing to stir, heat until it begins to boil. Reduce heat and simmer for 5 minutes, stirring. Remove from heat.

Cook pasta according to package directions; drain. Combine crabmeat, sherry, macaroni, artichokes and mushrooms with the sauce. Place in a large casserole dish. Sprinkle with Parmesan cheese and paprika. Bake at 350 degrees F. for 30 minutes.

Yield: 2 servings

Pasta Soups

Chicken Soup with Vermicelli

6 cups chicken stock
1 whole chicken breast, split
1/4 cup vegetable oil
1/4 lb. vermicelli, broken into 2-inch lengths
1 large tomato, skinned, seeded, and chopped
1 ripe avocado, peeled, pitted, and cut into chunks
2 hot green chilies, chopped
Salt and pepper to taste

At least 6 hours before serving, heat stock to boiling in a large saucepan. Add chicken, reduce heat to low, and simmer for 25 minutes.

Remove chicken from broth and set aside to cool. When chicken is cool enough to handle, remove skin and bones; shred chicken meat. Refrigerate chicken and stock until ready to use.

Heat vegetable oil in a small skillet. Add pasta and cook until lightly browned. Remove from saucepan and drain on paper towels.

Reheat stock to boiling. Add vermicelli and cook until tender. Add tomato and shredded chicken; heat thoroughly. Add avocado, chilies, salt and pepper; heat thorough. Serve soup piping hot.

Yield: 6 servings

Vegetable Soup

1 pkg. soup bones
2 tablespoons parsley flakes
1 teaspoon Kitchen Bouquet
1 tablespoon green bell pepper, chopped
1/8 teaspoon sweet basil
1 quart tomatoes
1/2 teaspoon oregano
3 bay leaves
1/8 teaspoon thyme
1/4 teaspoon Worcestershire sauce
Salt and pepper to taste
4 carrots, chopped
3 onions, chopped
1 1/2 cups celery, chopped
1 cup corn
1/3 cup elbow macaroni

Add soup bones to a large Dutch oven, cover with water and simmer for 3 hours. Remove bones from water, cool and clean meat from bones.

Return meat to pot and add parsley flakes, Kitchen Bouquet, bell pepper, sweet basil, tomatoes, oregano, bay leaves, thyme, Worcestershire sauce, salt and pepper. Simmer 1 hour. Add carrots, onions, celery, corn and macaroni. Cook until vegetables are tender.

Yield: 6 quarts

Slow Cooker Pasta Vegetable Soup

4 oz. rotini
32 oz. V-8 juice
1 (10 oz.) can low-sodium beef broth
3 carrots, sliced thin
2 stalks celery, sliced
2 tablespoons parsley flakes
1 clove garlic
1 1/4 teaspoon dried basil leaves
Salt and pepper to taste
8 oz. pkg. frozen green beans
1 (15 oz.) can kidney beans (with liquid)
3 links Italian sausage, cooked, drained and sliced
Parmesan cheese

Cook pasta according to package directions; drain.

Add V-8 juice, broth, carrots, celery, parsley, garlic, basil, salt, pepper, green beans and kidney beans to slow cooker; stir and cook on high until vegetables are done (4 hours.) Add meat and cook 15 to 20 minutes. Stir in cooked pasta. Garnish individual bowls with Parmesan cheese.

Yield: 4 servings

Minestrone Soup

4 slices bacon, chopped
1 cup onion, chopped
1/2 cup celery chopped,
3 cloves of garlic, minced
1 (10.5 oz.) can low-sodium beef broth
2 cups water
1 teaspoon basil
1 (20 oz.) can pork and beans
1 (16 oz.) can tomatoes, chopped
1/2 cup elbow macaroni
Salt and pepper to taste
1 cup zucchini, cubed
1 cup cabbage, shredded

Brown bacon with onion, celery and garlic in a large Dutch oven or soup pot. Add beef broth, water, basil, pork and beans, tomatoes with liquid, macaroni, salt and pepper.

Cover and simmer over low heat for 15 minutes, stirring occasionally. Add zucchini and cabbage; simmer for 10 to 15 minutes until vegetables are tender; stir occasionally.

Yield: 4 to 6 servings

Tortellini Soup

2 cloves garlic, minced
1 large onion, chopped
1 tablespoon olive oil
1 (14 1/2 to 16 oz.) can stewed tomatoes
3 (14.5 oz. each) cans low-sodium beef or chicken broth
1 teaspoon basil, crushed
1/2 to 3/4 cup picante sauce
7 oz. uncooked cheese tortellini
1 green bell pepper, diced
1 cup grated Parmesan cheese

In a large saucepan or Dutch oven, cook garlic and onion in oil until soft. Add tomatoes, broth, basil and picante sauce. Bring to a boil; stir in tortellini. Simmer, uncovered, for 15 minutes. Add green bell pepper; simmer 5 minutes. Pour into bowls and garnish with cheese.

Yield: 8 servings

Italian Sausage Soup

1 lb. bulk Italian sausage
1 cup onions, chopped
2 cloves garlic, minced
5 cups low-sodium beef broth
3/4 cup water
2 cups fresh or canned tomatoes, chopped
1 cup carrots, sliced
1/2 teaspoon oregano
1/2 teaspoon basil
1 (8 oz.) tomato sauce
1 1/2 cups zucchini, sliced
1 medium green bell pepper, chopped
3 tablespoons parsley, chopped
8 oz. small tortellini

In a large saucepan or Dutch oven, brown sausage. Add onions and garlic; cook until tender. Add beef broth, water, tomatoes, carrots, oregano, basil and tomato sauce; bring to a boil.

Lower heat and simmer 30 minutes. Skim fat from top. Stir in zucchini, bell pepper, parsley and tortellini. Simmer, covered, for 35 minutes or until pasta is tender.

Yield: 9 servings

Pasta and Bean Soup

1/4 cup olive oil
1 tablespoon onion, minced
2 cloves garlic, crushed
1 1/2 cans (8 oz. each) tomato sauce
8 to 10 cups water
2 (15.5 oz. each) cans dark red kidney beans
2 tablespoons Adobo seasoning
3/4 tablespoon Parmesan cheese
1/2 stick pepperoni, sliced
1/2 lb. hot sausage, diced
8 oz. macaroni

In a large saucepan or Dutch oven, sauté olive oil, onion and garlic. Add tomato sauce, water, kidney beans, Adobo seasoning, cheese, pepperoni and hot sausage. Simmer for 1 hour.

Cook pasta according to package directions; drain.

Mix pasta and soup in bowls.

Yield: 6 servings

Pepperoni Bow Tie Soup

7 cups low-sodium beef broth
1 (14.5 oz.) can Italian style stewed tomatoes
1 medium onion, sliced
1 medium carrot, sliced
1 (9 oz.) pkg. frozen Italian green beans
1 large zucchini, halved lengthwise and sliced
1 tablespoon dried Italian seasoning
1/2 cup bow tie pasta
1 (3.5 oz.) pkg. pepperoni, sliced
Garlic salt, to taste
Grated Parmesan cheese
Black pepper, to taste

In a Dutch oven or large saucepan, combine broth, tomatoes, onions, carrots, green beans, zucchini and Italian seasoning; bring to a boil. Reduce heat and simmer, partially covered for 20 minutes. Add pasta and simmer uncovered for 15 minutes, stirring occasionally until pasta is cooked. Stir in pepperoni and heat through. Season with salt and pepper. Garnish individual portions with cheese.

Yield: 6 servings

Chunky Pork Soup

3 slices bacon, cooked until crisp
1 cup celery, sliced 1/4-inch thick
1 cup carrots, sliced 1/4-inch thick
1/2 cup onion, chopped
2 to 3 cups cooked ham or pork, cubed
1 (28 oz.) can tomatoes, chopped
2 cups water
2 small zucchini, 1/2-inch chunks
1 cup rotini pasta
1 teaspoon dried basil
1 teaspoon dried thyme
1/4 teaspoon garlic salt
1/4 teaspoon pepper
Grated Parmesan cheese
Snipped parsley

Sauté celery, carrots and onion until tender in a stock pot.
Add ham or pork, tomatoes, water, zucchini, pasta, basil,
thyme, garlic salt and pepper. Simmer 15 to 20 minutes.
Garnish with parsley, Parmesan cheese and crumbled
bacon.

Yield: 4 servings

Hearty Minestrone Soup

1 lb. lean hamburger
2 carrots, sliced
1 large onion, chopped
2 or 3 stalks celery, sliced
2 (14.5 oz. each) cans Italian tomatoes, chopped
1 box frozen spinach, chopped
1 cup elbow macaroni, uncooked
1/2 teaspoon pepper
1/2 teaspoon basil
1/2 teaspoon salt
1/2 teaspoon oregano
3 (14.5 oz. each) cans low-sodium beef broth
1 (15 oz.) can garbanzo beans, drained
1 (15.5 oz.) can red beans, drained

Brown hamburger in large pot; drain. Add carrots, onion, celery, tomatoes, spinach, macaroni, pepper, basil, salt, oregano, beef broth, garbanzo beans and red beans. Simmer on low 30 minutes or longer.

Yield: 6 servings

Pasta Salads and Side Dishes

Vermicelli Salad with Crabmeat

8 oz. vermicelli
8 black Chinese dried mushrooms
1 lb. crabmeat
4 scallions, sliced
1 cup water chestnuts, drained and cut into thin strips
1 cup bamboo shoots, drained and cut into thin strips
2 tablespoons soy sauce
2 tablespoons sweet and sour sauce
3 drops hot chili sauce
3 tablespoons oil
3 tablespoons lemon juice

Cook pasta according to package directions until al dente; drain.

Place mushrooms in bowl and cover with boiling water; let soak for 30 minutes. Drain and cut into strips.

In a large bowl, combine pasta, mushrooms, crabmeat, scallions, water chestnuts, bamboo shoots, soy sauce, sweet and sour sauce, chili sauce, and oil; mix well. Sprinkle salad with lemon juice, and serve.

Yield: 4 servings

Light and Easy Pasta Salad

2 cups (8 oz.) rotini pasta
2/3 cup reduced calorie Italian dressing
1 cup halved cherry tomatoes
2 cups halved zucchini slices
1 cup sliced mushrooms
1 cup (4 oz.) reduced fat Cheddar cheese, shredded
2 tablespoons Parmesan cheese

Cook pasta according to package directions; drain.

Mix Italian dressing with tomatoes, zucchini, mushrooms
and pasta; cover. Chill several hours. Toss with Cheddar
cheese. Serve on a lettuce leaf-lined platter and sprinkle
with Parmesan cheese.

Yield: 6 servings

Pizza Salad

8 oz. rotini
1 lb. diced cheese, mild or sharp Cheddar
3 tomatoes, chopped, seeded
1 to 2 bunches scallions, sliced
3 oz. pepperoni, sliced

Dressing:
3/4 cup olive oil
1/2 cup red wine vinegar (or white vinegar)
2/3 cup Parmesan cheese
2 teaspoons dried oregano
1 teaspoon garlic powder
Salt and pepper
Croutons

Cook pasta according to package directions; drain. In a large bowl, combine rotini, cheese, tomatoes, scallions and pepperoni.

Mix oil with vinegar, Parmesan cheese, oregano, garlic powder, salt and pepper; pour over pasta mixture. Chill 4 hours; Toss and garnish with croutons.

Yield: 4 servings

Fire and Ice Pasta Salad

1 lb. rotini or spaghetti
1/2 cup olive oil
1/4 teaspoon chili flakes
1 garlic clove, crushed, minced
1 teaspoon salt
1/4 teaspoon pepper
2 lb. tomatoes (about 6), diced
1/4 cup chopped fresh basil
1/4 cup chopped fresh parsley
2 tablespoons chopped fresh chives

Cook pasta according to package directions; drain.

Blend olive oil with chili flakes, garlic, salt and pepper. Mix with tomatoes, basil, parsley and chives. Let stand at room temperature, covered, for 20 minutes to 1 hour. Toss with pasta and serve.

Yield: 4 to 6 servings

Best Pasta Salad

8 oz. rotini pasta
1 large tomato, chopped
1 medium red bell pepper, chopped
1 can black olives, sliced
1 medium green bell pepper, chopped
1 small onion, chopped
1/4 cup Parmesan cheese
1 (8 oz.) bottle sun dried tomato vinaigrette dressing

Cook pasta according to package directions; drain and rinse in cold water.

Mix tomato, bell pepper, olives, bell pepper and onion. Add pasta and chill one hour; mix with salad dressing. Toss with Parmesan cheese.

Yield: 4 servings

Greek Rotini Salad

1 (12 oz.) pkg. rotini, tricolor
1 cup feta cheese, Roquefort or blue cheese, crumbled
1/2 cup black olives, coarsely chopped
3/4 cup radishes, sliced
1/4 cup green onion, sliced
1 small cucumber, thinly sliced

Dressing:
1/2 cup olive oil or vegetable oil
2 tablespoons lemon juice
2 tablespoons fresh parsley, chopped
1 clove garlic, minced
1 teaspoon Italian seasoning
1 teaspoon lemon pepper, or lemon and herb seasoning
1 teaspoon basil

Cook pasta according to package directions; drain. In a large bowl, toss hot cooked rotini with cheese, olives, radishes, onions and cucumber.

In a small bowl, combine oil with lemon juice, parsley, garlic, Italian seasoning, lemon pepper and basil; toss with pasta mix and add salt and pepper as needed. Refrigerate 1 to 2 hours before serving.

Yield: 6 to 8 servings

Penne Pasta Salad

1 lb. penne pasta
1 red bell pepper, julienned
1 bunch scallions or green onions
1 bunch asparagus, cooked, chopped in 1-inch pieces
1 (13.75) can artichoke hearts
1/4 cup olive oil
10 sun-dried tomatoes, chopped
8 oz. feta cheese, cubed
1 (8 oz.) bottle vinaigrette salad dressing
2 cloves garlic, chopped
2 tablespoons pesto (optional)

Cook pasta according to package directions; drain. Sauté bell pepper in a little olive oil. Mix all ingredients and chill in covered container. Toss before serving.

Yield: 6 - 8 servings

Piquant Vermicelli

8 oz. vermicelli
1/4 cup butter
1/4 lb. mushrooms, thinly sliced
1 teaspoon marjoram
2 tablespoons chopped parsley
Salt and pepper to taste

Cook pasta according to package directions; drain. Place in serving bowl and keep warm.

Melt butter in a small saucepan. Add mushrooms; cook over low heat stirring constantly for 3 minutes. Spoon mushrooms over vermicelli. Add marjoram, parsley, salt and pepper; toss until well mixed. Serve at once.

Yield: 6 servings

Rigatoni Salad

1 (16 oz. pkg.) rigatoni
1 cup granulated sugar
1 teaspoon salt
1 teaspoon Accent
1 teaspoon garlic powder
1 cup vegetable oil
1 cup vinegar
1 teaspoon pepper
1 teaspoon parsley flakes
1 cucumber, diced
1 medium onion, diced

Cook pasta according to directions on package; drain.

In a medium bowl, combine sugar, salt, Accent, garlic powder, vegetable oil, vinegar, pepper and parsley.

Combine seasoned oil with pasta, onion and cucumber. Refrigerate at least 48 hours. Stir occasionally.

Yield: 6 to 8 servings

Cashew Tortellini Chicken Salad

2 cups cheese tortellini
2 cups frozen sugar snap peas
2 cups cooked chicken, diced
1/4 cup celery, chopped
3 tablespoons green onions, sliced
1 tablespoon pimientos, chopped
1/4 teaspoon salt
1/2 cup reduced fat ranch dressing
1/4 cup whole cashews
Leaf lettuce

Cook pasta according to directions on package; drain and rinse with cold water.

Thaw sugar snap peas in water; drain. In a large bowl, combine chicken, celery, green onions, pimientos, salt and snap peas. Pour dressing over salad; mix to coat. Refrigerate at least 2 to 3 hours. Serve on lettuce leaf and garnish with cashews.

Yield: 2 servings

Shrimp Salad

1 (7 oz.) pkg. elbow macaroni
2 hard cooked eggs, chopped
1 cup celery, chopped
2 (4 oz. each) cans shrimp
1/8 cup green bell pepper, chopped
1 green onion, sliced
1 tablespoon pimento

Dressing:

1 cup salad dressing or mayonnaise
3 tablespoons cream

Cook pasta according to directions on package; rinse, drain and cool.

In a large bowl, mix macaroni, eggs, celery, shrimp, bell pepper, onion and pimento. Add dressing and toss to coat evenly.

Yield: 12 servings

Green Tomato Pasta

4 cups spaghetti
4 large green tomatoes, thinly sliced (1/8-inch thick)
Salt and pepper, to taste
1 cup flour
Vegetable oil, for frying
2 garlic cloves, minced
1/4 cup parmesan cheese, grated

Prepare spaghetti according to package directions; drain well and set aside.

Season tomatoes with salt and pepper. Coat with flour and fry in hot oil with garlic until golden brown. Do not overcook. Place fried tomato slices on top of hot, cooked pasta. Top with parmesan cheese and serve immediately.

Yield: 4 servings

Ham, Peas and Cheese Salad

1 (7 oz.) pkg. elbow macaroni
1 (10 oz.) pkg. frozen peas
1 cup cheddar cheese, cubed
2 cups cooked ham, cubed
1 cup salad dressing (not mayonnaise)
2 tablespoons onions, minced
3/4 teaspoon salt
1/4 teaspoon pepper
1 teaspoon lemon juice

Cook pasta according to directions on package; rinse, drain and cool.

Cover peas with boiling water, but do not cook. Let peas stand in hot water 5 minutes; drain. Mix macaroni and peas, cheese and ham.

In a small bowl, blend dressing, onion, salt, pepper and lemon juice. Pour dressing over macaroni mix and toss gently to coat. Refrigerate at least one hour.

Yield: 4 servings

Shrimp Salad

Mix together:

1 (7 oz.) pkg. medium shell pasta (cooked, rinsed and drained)
1 (12 oz.) pkg. little frozen shrimp
1 cup celery, chopped
3/4 cup frozen peas
Diced cheese

Set aside.

Dressing:

1/3 cup granulated sugar
1/3 cup vegetable oil
1 cup mayonnaise
1/4 cup ketchup
1/4 cup vinegar
1 teaspoon dry mustard
1/4 teaspoon paprika
1 medium onion, chopped
1/4 teaspoon salt
Garlic salt and pepper to taste

In a small bowl, mix dressing ingredients and toss with macaroni mixture. Add garlic salt and pepper to taste. Dressing is thin, but it thickens when chilled.

Yield: 4 servings

Armenian Pilaf

6 tablespoons butter or margarine
1 1/2 cups broken pieces vermicelli
1 cup rice
1/2 teaspoon salt
2 cups boiling water

In a large saucepan, melt butter or margarine; add vermicelli. Cook over medium-high heat, stirring until well browned. Add rice, salt and boiling water; stir and cover. Boil slowly for 10 minutes.

Remove from heat and let stand covered for 15 to 20 minutes. Keep warm in oven if not served immediately.

Yield: 6 servings

Ham and Macaroni Salad

2 cups elbow macaroni
1/2 lb. boiled or baked ham, diced
1/2 cup cheddar cheese, diced
1 small onion, chopped
1 cup celery, chopped
1/2 cup dill pickle, diced
1/2 cup mayonnaise
2 teaspoons prepared mustard
Lettuce leaves
3 to 6 hard-boiled eggs, sliced
3 tomatoes, quartered

Cook pasta according to directions on package; drain. In a medium bowl, combine ham, cheese, onion, celery and pickles with macaroni.

Mix mayonnaise with mustard and stir into macaroni mixture; chill until ready to serve. Serve spooned onto lettuce leaves and garnished with eggs and tomatoes.

Yield: 6 servings

Acini De Pepe Pasta Fruit Salad

1 cup granulated sugar
2 tablespoons flour
1/2 teaspoon salt
1 3/4 cups pineapple juice
2 eggs, beaten
1 tablespoon lemon juice
1 (16 oz.) pkg. acini de pepe pasta
3 (11 oz. each) cans mandarin oranges, drained
2 (20 oz. each) cans pineapple chunks, drained
1 (20 oz.) can crushed pineapple, drained
1 (8 oz.) Cool Whip
1 cup flaked coconut, optional
2 cups miniature marshmallows, optional

Combine sugar, flour and salt in a small saucepan. Stir in pineapple juice and eggs. Stirring constantly, simmer over moderate heat until thickened. Blend in lemon juice; cool sauce to room temperature.

Cook pasta according to directions on package; drain, rinse in cold water, drain again. Gently blend egg mix and macaroni. Refrigerate overnight in sealed container.

The next morning, add fruit, Cool Whip, coconut and marshmallows. Fold gently to incorporate ingredients. Refrigerate in sealed container until chilled. Prepare 24 hours before serving.

Note: Fresh fruit can be substituted for canned.

Yield: 25 servings

Macaroni Fruit Salad

1/2 pkg. elbow macaroni
1 large apple, diced
1/2 jar maraschino cherries and juice, quartered
1/2 pkg. small marshmallows
1/2 cup crushed pineapple with juice
1/2 cup granulated sugar or sugar substitute
1/2 cup lemon juice
2 eggs, beaten
1 tablespoon flour
1/2 pint fat free nondairy whipped topping

Cook pasta according to package directions; rinse, drain and cool. Combine apple, macaroni, cherries, marshmallows and pineapple in a large bowl.

In a small saucepan, mix sugar, lemon juice, eggs and flour, cooking and stirring until bubbling; cool and mix into salad. Refrigerate overnight. Before serving, add 1/2 pint nondairy whipped topping to salad.

Yield: 3 to 4 servings

Italian Pasta Salad

1 lb. small shell pasta
4 oz. provolone cheese, chopped
4 oz. salami, chopped
4 oz. pepperoni, chopped
2 small onions, chopped
1/2 cup celery, chopped
1/2 cup green bell pepper, chopped
1/2 cup red bell pepper, chopped
1 (2.25) can pitted black olives, chopped
1 (7 oz.) jar green olives, chopped
3 to 5 ripe tomatoes, chopped
Fresh parsley to taste

Dressing:
3/4 cup olive oil
1/2 cup white vinegar
1 tablespoon salt
1 teaspoon pepper
3 tablespoons granulated sugar
1 tablespoon oregano

Cook pasta according to package directions; drain. In a large bowl, combine with cheese, salami, pepperoni, onions, celery, green bell pepper, red bell pepper, black olives and green olives.

In a small bowl, combine olive oil, vinegar, sugar, oregano, salt and pepper. Gently toss with salad and chill for 24 hours. Add the tomatoes and parsley just before serving.

Yield: 15 servings

Macaroni and Chicken Salad

1 (16 oz.) pkg. elbow macaroni
1/2 cup reduced fat French dressing
1 1/3 cups reduced fat mayonnaise
1 chicken, cooked and cut into bite-size pieces
1 teaspoon salt
1/2 green bell pepper, chopped
2 cups celery, sliced
2/3 cup sweet pickle relish
2 tablespoons onions, minced

Cook pasta according to package directions; drain and cool.
Blend French dressing with mayonnaise; mix in chicken,
salt, bell pepper, celery, relish and onion. Mix with
macaroni. Chill.

Yield: 8 servings

Spring Salad with Shell Pasta

1 (16 oz.) pkg. small shell pasta
1 large cucumber, diced
1 onion, chopped fine
3 medium carrots, grated
3 ribs celery, sliced thin
1 green bell pepper, chopped

Dressing:

2 cups reduced fat mayonnaise
1 cup granulated sugar
1 cup white vinegar
1 (14 oz.) can fat free sweetened condensed milk

Cook pasta according to package directions; drain. Combine pasta with vegetables in a large bowl. Pour dressing over ingredients and toss to coat.

Yield: 12 to 15 servings

Smoked Turkey and Pepper Pasta Salad

8 oz. fettuccine
3/4 cup reduced fat Miracle Whip
1 tablespoon Dijon mustard
1/2 teaspoon dried thyme
1 cup (8 oz.) smoked turkey breast, diced
3/4 cup zucchini slices, halved
1/2 cup red bell pepper strips
1/2 cup yellow bell pepper strips
Salt and pepper to taste

Cook fettuccine according to package directions; drain and rinse.

Mix salad dressing, mustard and thyme until well blended. Add pasta, turkey, zucchini, red and yellow bell pepper strips; mix lightly. Season with salt and pepper to taste. Chill for 4 hours.

Yield: 4 servings

Hearty Macaroni Salad

2 cups ham, cubed
2 cups cooked chicken, cubed
2 cups cooked salad shrimp
1 (7 oz.) pkg. elbow macaroni
2 cups celery, chopped
1/4 cup green bell pepper, diced
1/4 cup sweet red bell pepper, diced
1/2 cup onion diced
1 teaspoon salt
1/2 teaspoon pepper

Toss all ingredients together in a large bowl.

Dressing:

1/2 cup light mayonnaise
1/2 cup reduced fat sour cream
2 teaspoons vinegar
1/2 teaspoon granulated sugar
2 teaspoons fresh dill, minced

In a small bowl, mix dressing ingredients; pour on salad and gently toss to blend. Cover. Chill 3 to 4 hours.

Yield: 12 servings

Tomato Spaghetti Salad

2 (16 oz. each) pkg. spaghetti
3 to 4 tomatoes, chopped
2 large green bell peppers, chopped
1 large onion, chopped

Dressing:

1 1/2 cup granulated sugar
2 cups olive oil
2/3 cup apple cider vinegar
2 tablespoons yellow mustard
2 tablespoons salt
1 tablespoon poppy seeds

Cook spaghetti according to package directions; drain, but do not rinse. Add tomatoes, bell peppers and onion. Mix dressing ingredients and pour over spaghetti and vegetables. Refrigerate overnight.

Yield: 6 to 8 servings

Other books by Victoria Steele:

101 Quick & Easy Cupcake and Muffin Recipes

101 Quick & Easy Cookie Recipes

101 Quick & Easy Chicken Recipes

101 Quick & Easy 5 Ingredient Recipes

101 Quick & Easy Italian Recipes

Printed in Great Britain
by Amazon

18967720R00068